AF481065

Did the Vikings Really Wear Horned Helmets in Battles?

History Book Best Sellers
Children's History

In this book, we're going to talk about the Vikings and their battles. So, let's get right to it!

Frank Brangwyn
1883

WHO WERE THE VIKINGS?

Beginning in 800 AD, people from the Scandinavian countries of Denmark and Norway as well as Sweden traveled on boats to go to other regions of Europe. They stole, plundered, and murdered on these raids and terrorized wherever they went. These raids occurred between 800 AD and 1066 AD so this time period was named the Viking Age.

THE HORNED HELMET

Whenever we see illustrations of Vikings today, they are often shown with horned helmets. The Vikings did wear helmets in battle but they more than likely didn't wear any that had horns. The horns were an invention of illustrators in the 1800s that were painting depictions of their epic battles. Costume designers loved the look and created these helmets for stage characters, so a stereotype was born.

THE VIKING RAIDS

"Viking" came from the verb "to raid" in the language of Old Norse. In their long, streamlined ships, the Vikings would travel across the seas to plunder villages on the northern coast of Europe. Their conquests included the island lands that eventually became Great Britain as well as Scotland.

Their first attack in England was in 787 AD. They brutally attacked wealthy monasteries, where religious

monks lived. Because the monks had no way to defend themselves, the Vikings easily stole from them.

EARLY RAIDS

In 793 AD, the Vikings attacked the Lindisfarne Monastery that was located on Britain's coast. These Vikings most likely traveled from the lands that are now the country of Norway. They didn't completely level the monastery, however the news that a monastery had suffered an attack sent widespread fear across the mostly Christian countries of Europe.

Lindisfarne Monastery

Saint-Philibert

At that time, the Vikings were pagans and didn't respect the beliefs of Christianity.

Two years later, in 795 AD, they raided the islands of Iona, as well as Rathlin and Skye off the coast of Scotland.

In 799 AD, they raided St. Philibert's Monastery, which was located on Noirmoutier Island off France's coast.

INLAND RAIDS

As news spread regarding unrest in Europe, the Vikings got even bolder and started to make raids on lands that were inland from the coasts. Rulers of some of the Germanic tribes decided to use the widespread fear of the Vikings to their advantage.

Lothar 1

They paid them not to attack their lands and some of them even gained the support of the Vikings in their regional wars. In 840 AD, Lothar I, a ruler from the Frankish Kingdoms, invited a fleet of Vikings to help him regain power from his brothers. Payments from wealthy kingdoms made the Vikings quite well off and added to their power.

LATER RAIDS

During the 9th century, the Vikings continued their raids of terror throughout the European continent.

In 842 AD, they raided Nantes, a city in the Frankish Kingdoms. They then traveled up the Loire River and began systematic attacks on a number of inland cities including Paris, Orleans, and Nimes.

Loire River

Alexandria, Egypt

In 844 AD, they stormed the city of Seville in what is now Spain, which was controlled by the Arabs at that time.

In 859 AD, they left the coast of France traveling in 62 ships. They started to raid cities along the coast of the Mediterranean including Pisa in the country of Italy. It's thought that they may have traveled as far as the city of Alexandria in Egypt.

THE SETTLING OF NORMANDY

A Frankish king named Charles the Simple gave some land to Rollo who was a Viking leader. For this exchange, Charles asked that the Vikings keep other traders from using the Seine River for transportation. The land that Rollo ruled was called Normandy. The word Normandy means "Land of Northmen."

Rollo

Charles the Simple

THE BRITISH ISLES

By the middle of the 9th century, the Vikings had seized most of the lands we now know as Scotland as well as its islands to the north. They had founded several of Ireland's towns, such as Dublin, Wexford, and Limerick. These towns were used as their bases so they could attack inland cities of Ireland and travel across the Irish Sea to attack England.

Danish Vikings attacked East Anglia as well as Northumberland. In England, King Alfred the Great was able to defeat them at Wessex. When they lost Wessex, the Danish Vikings settled further north

and established a city, which they called Danelaw. Some became traders and farmers and they started the city of York as a trading hub.

Eric Bloodaxe

K ing Alfred's descendants took back the parts of England that the Vikings had captured in the 10th century. They killed Erik Bloodaxe, the last Viking Scandinavian King, in the year 952 AD. After they defeated the Vikings, they were able to unify the kingdom of England once more.

WESTWARD EXPANSION

The Vikings had amazing navigational and seafaring skills. They began to travel across the Atlantic. They built settlements in both Iceland and Greenland. Some Vikings led by Leif Eriksson who was the son of Viking leader Erik the Red, traveled all the way to North America.

Christopher Columbus

They named it Vinland and constructed a town there that is now Newfoundland in Canada. This was in the 11th century, hundreds of years before Christopher Columbus set foot in the New World.

THE SECOND VIKING AGE

The Viking Harald Bluetooth was known for his communication skills and ability to negotiate. He brought Norway and Denmark together and ruled the countries between 940 AD and 986 AD. Ultimately he brought all of Scandinavia together. He also influenced the conversion of the Danes to the Christian religion. With the support of royal leaders, the Vikings began new raids on the English coastline.

Edward the Confessor

S ven Forkbeard was a Viking conqueror who led these new raids on England. He was able to conquer the whole kingdom in the year 1013 AD. After Sven passed away, his son Canute, also spelled Knut, ruled an empire of the countries of Denmark along with Norway and England.

This empire was short-lived. Edward the Confessor took back England's lands and his successors were able to fight off further attacks from the Vikings. At York, they defeated Harald Hardrad who was the last great Viking king.

THE NORMAN CONQUEST

All the battles with the Vikings had made the English armies very weak. A few weeks after the battle that took place at York, William the Conqueror, who was a descendant of settlers from Scandinavia and who was also the Duke of Normandy, marched in and took over England.

William the Conqueror

William the Conqueror's Castle

This event marked the end of the age of the Vikings. William was able to keep the country safe. By that time, the kingdoms of Scandinavia had become mostly Christian.

THE VIKING SHIPS

The Vikings had amazing ships that they built out of long planks of wood. They overlapped the wood's edges to make the ships. Most of the ships they traveled in were called longships.

Viking Ships

These boats were long, rather narrow, and very streamlined. Oars were used to propel the boat forward and sometimes, if it was windy, a sail was also used. The boats were built so they floated in very shallow water, which made them perfect for beach landings.

F or trading, the Vikings built special
cargo ships. Each ship was called a
knarr. These knarrer ships were deeper
and also wider so that they were the right
size for carrying cargo.

In Denmark, there's a museum that
houses five actual ships from the Vikings.
There's a display that shows exactly how
the ships were made.

Viking Ship "Hugin"

LANGUAGE INFLUENCES

Throughout England as well as Russia and Scotland the language of the Vikings can be seen in many place names and words. The suffix "by" means town and in the Yorkshire region of England over 200 names of towns carry that suffix. Grimsby, which means Grimr's town and Wetherby, which means ram's town.

Many words in the English language are derived from the Old Norse—egg, creek, and plow are just a few of many examples.

VIKING CULTURE AND RELIGION

The Vikings practiced a type of paganism. Later in their history they converted to Christianity. They were fine craftsmen and artists and added decorations to the swords they used for fighting as well as fine jewelry.

FASCINATING FACTS ABOUT VIKINGS

B luetooth technology, which is a modern communication method, is named after Harald Bluetooth. It isn't known for certain if he was nicknamed Bluetooth because of his communication skills or because he actually had a bluetooth. The logo for the company is a design made with runes, which are ancient Norse letters.

❖ Vikings sometimes used enormous axes with two handles in battle. They could cut apart metal helmets or protective shields.

❖ Vikings living in the country of Ireland formed the very first parliament.

❖ The city of Dublin in Ireland was begun by Vikings.

❖ Vikings were sometimes hired as bodyguards for emperors.

❖ The Minnesota NFL team has a Viking as its mascot.

A wesome! Now you know more about the Vikings. You can find more History books from Baby Professor by searching the website of your favorite book retailer.

Visit

BABY PROFESSOR
EDUCATION KIDS

www.BabyProfessorBooks.com

to download Free Baby Professor eBooks and view
our catalog of new and exciting Children's Books

www.ingramcontent.com/pod-product-compliance
Lightning Source LLC
Chambersburg PA
CBHW080542110726
47973CB00005B/64